101 ESSENTIAL TIPS

Cooking with
SPICES

ESSENTIAL TIPS
101

Cooking with
SPICES

Jill Norman

DK PUBLISHING, INC.

www.dk.com

A DK PUBLISHING BOOK

www.dk.com

Editor Polly Boyd
Art Editor Mason Linklater
Senior Editor Gillian Roberts
Series Art Editor Alison Donovan
Production Controller Jenny May
US Editors Jill Hamilton, Ray Rogers

Recipes for Tips 67, 72, 77, 84, 87, 88 by Anne Willan
Recipes for all other tips by Jill Norman

**Follow either imperial or metric units throughout a recipe,
never a mixture of the two, since they are not exact equivalents.**

First American Edition 1998
4 6 8 10 9 7 5
Published in the United States by DK Publishing, Inc.
95 Madison Avenue, New York, New York 10016

ISBN 0-7894-2778-8

Text film output by R&B Creative Services Ltd, Great Britain
Reproduced by Colourscan, Singapore
Printed in China by WKT

ESSENTIAL TIPS

PAGES 8–12

SPICE KNOW-HOW

1 ....What are spices?
2 ....Aroma & taste
3 ....Selecting spices
4 ....How to grind spices
5 ....How to bruise spices
6 ....How to dry-roast spices
7 ....Kitchen pepper
8 ....Storing dried spices
9 ....Storing fresh spices
10 ....Freezing spices

PAGES 13–37

SPICE PROFILES

11 ....Cooking with spices
12 ....Dill
13 ....Celery
14 ....Mustard
15 ....Mustard products
16 ....Prepared mustards
17 ....Chilies
18 ....Fresh chilies
19 ....Dried chilies
20 ....Chili products
21 ....Using chilies safely
22 ....Making chili oil
23 ....Chilies as a garnish
24 ....Paprika
25 ....Caraway
26 ....Cassia
27 ....Cinnamon
28 ....Kaffir lime
29 ....Coriander & cilantro
30 ....Saffron
31 ....How to use saffron
32 ....Cumin
33 ....Turmeric
34 ....Lemongrass
35 ....How to use lemongrass
36 ....Cardamom

37 ....Cloves
38 ....Asafetida
39 ....Using fresh asafetida
40 ....Fennel
41 ....Star anise
42 ....Juniper
43 ....Galangal
44 ....Curry leaves
45 ....Nutmeg & mace
46 ....Spiced vinegar
47 ....Nigella
48 ....Poppy
49 ....Allspice
50 ....Anise
51 ....Pepper
52 ....Cubeb
53 ....Sumac
54 ....Sesame
55 ....Tamarind
56 ....Fenugreek
57 ....Vanilla
58 ....Sichuan pepper
59 ....Ginger
60 ....How to prepare fresh ginger

PAGES 38–44

FAR EAST

61 ....Thai shrimp soup with
lemongrass
62 ....Seven-spice powder
63 ....Chicken with noodles
64 ....Sea bass with star anise
65 ....Five-spice powder
66 ....Thai red curry paste
67 ....Beef curry
68 ....Chicken satay
69 ....Peanut sauce

PAGES 45–51

INDIA

70......................................Fruit chat
71...............................Chat masala
72................Mixed vegetable curry
73............................Curry powder
74..................................Lime pickle
75..............................Garam masala
76...............Aromatic cold chicken
77............................Spicy fish stew

PAGES 52–57

NORTH AFRICA & MIDDLE EAST

78..Harissa
79..............................Ras el hanout
80..................................Harira
81...............................Spiced olives
82..................................Falafel
83............................Fish couscous
84...............Moroccan spicy chicken
85...................................Arab bread

PAGES 58–64

EUROPE

86............Mussel soup with saffron
87............................Country terrine
88............Mushrooms à la grecque
89.................Potatoes with juniper
90......................Venison with green
                                    peppercorns
91.............................Quatre épices
92.................................Mixed spice
93................................Mulled wine
94...................Gingerbread cookies

PAGES 65–69

THE AMERICAS & CARIBBEAN

95.............Ceviche (marinated fish)
96.......................Marinated shrimp
97..........................Cajun seasoning
98....................Louisiana dirty rice
99........................Bolivian corn pie
100............Jamaican jerk seasoning
101.........................Jerked chicken

INDEX 70
ACKNOWLEDGMENTS 72

SPICE KNOW-HOW

1 WHAT ARE SPICES?

Spices are strongly flavored or aromatic substances of vegetable origin – seeds, roots, leaves, bark, buds, and berries and other fruits – often used as flavorings. In ancient times, they were used as preservatives, medicines, and perfumes; the Romans were the first to use large quantities in cooking. Spices were once a rare and exotic luxury for the wealthy. Today, you can choose from a range of spices that is the widest ever known.

△ LEAVES
Some plants, such as kaffir lime (above), cilantro, dill, and fennel, have aromatic leaves that may be used in cooking to flavor foods.

△ BUDS
The dried, unripe fruits of cassia (above) are used in pickles in the Far East. Cloves are the unopened flower buds of a small evergreen tree.

◁ OILS
Essential oils distilled from certain plants are used more for medicinal purposes and in commercial food preparation than at home. This ginger oil flavors wines, beers, and cordials.

△ ROOTS
Ginger and galangal (above) are often used in root form. Turmeric, another root, is usually sold ground in the West.

△ SEEDS
Numerous spices are available in seed form – cardamom (above), cumin, coriander, fennel, poppy, and mustard. Many are native to the Mediterranean basin.

▷ BERRIES & FRUITS
Peppercorns (right), Sichuan pepper, juniper, allspice, cubeb, and sumac are all berries. Chilies are the fruits of plants in the genus Capsicum.

◁ BARK
Both cinnamon (left) and cassia are the dried bark of trees of the laurel family. They are very similar to each other.

2 AROMA & TASTE

Spices are often described as being either "aromatic" or "pungent." Some spices, such as cinnamon or nutmeg, are aromatic without heat; others, such as chilies, are pungent with little aroma; most are in between. A distinct anise flavor is characteristic of many spices.

▽ PUNGENT: FRESH CHILIES

△ AROMATIC: NUTMEG

3 SELECTING SPICES

Buy seeds and dried berries and other fruits as whole spices: they keep their flavor and aroma much longer than when ground. Avoid cracked or hollow fruits and pods. Check that fresh spices are not moldy, and dried ones are not faded or musty smelling.

4 HOW TO GRIND SPICES

Grinding or crushing spices releases their flavor and aroma. Most spices, including turmeric, mace, dried ginger, cassia, and cinnamon, are easy to grind. There are many ways of grinding spices, shown below. Whichever method you choose, grind them as needed rather than in advance to preserve their full flavor.

▷ PEPPER MILL
Some spices, such as coriander, allspice, and fenugreek, grind well in a pepper mill.

▽ MORTAR & PESTLE
Pounding spices in a mortar and pestle is the traditional method. It is ideal for grinding small quantities.

◁ ELECTRIC GRINDER
A coffee grinder is a quick and effective way to grind spices, particularly in large quantities. For spice pastes, use a food processor.

5 HOW TO BRUISE SPICES

Some spices, such as juniper berries, cardamom pods, dried ginger, and fresh lemongrass, should be lightly crushed to release their flavor, not ground. Place the spices in a bag or envelope and tap them with a rolling pin, or press lightly with a pestle in a mortar.

LIGHTLY BRUISING JUNIPER BERRIES

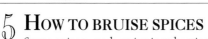

6 HOW TO DRY-ROAST SPICES

Dry-roasting certain spices – cumin, coriander, cardamom, and others – brings out their full flavor and aroma, and is essential in Indian cookery. After roasting, take the spices off the heat and allow to cool before grinding.

DRY-ROASTING CARDAMOM SEEDS
Remove the seeds from the pods. Heat a heavy skillet and add the seeds. Roast, stirring frequently until they give off an aroma, but do not let them scorch.

7 KITCHEN PEPPER

Nineteenth-century cookbooks often included recipes for kitchen pepper, a blend of peppers and other spices made up to suit the cook. Black, white, and dried green peppercorns form the base. Add cubebs (*Tip 52*) if you like a sharp piquancy or, for a more fragrant blend, use allspice, coriander, or cloves. Store in a pepper mill.

8 STORING DRIED SPICES

Store dried spices in airtight containers in a cool, dry place: heat, light, and moisture will impair their flavor. Whole spices will keep for several months in the right conditions, or even up to a year. Ground spices, however, lose their flavor within a few months. Check spices regularly, and replace any that smell stale.

△ **GLASS JARS**
Store spices in transparent containers in a cool cupboard. Direct light will cause them to fade and lose their flavor.

◁ **CERAMIC CONTAINERS**
Spices in solid containers may be stored on open shelves, but keep them away from hot or steamy areas.

9 STORING FRESH SPICES

Galangal, fresh ginger, and chilies will keep for two to three weeks in the refrigerator. Lemongrass, curry leaves, and kaffir lime leaves will keep for about one week in the crisper in the refrigerator. Fresh cilantro is best bought as you need it, since it keeps for only three to four days. If you need to store it, place the stem-ends in a jar of water, or wrap it in paper towels and place it in a plastic bag in the refrigerator.

△ GINGER IN SHERRY
To keep fresh ginger for several months, peel, slice, and bottle it in dry sherry.

▽ FRESH GINGER
Wrap ginger and galangal in paper towels before refrigerating. This absorbs moisture, which causes rot.

▽ FRESH LEMONGRASS
Place lemongrass, kaffir lime leaves, and curry leaves in a sealed plastic bag with a little moisture and air, and refrigerate.

10 FREEZING SPICES

Many fresh spices freeze well. This is particularly useful for spices that are difficult to obtain. To freeze fresh ginger and galangal, peel the root and keep it in a covered plastic container in the freezer. To use, grate what you need from the frozen root, then return it to the freezer. For fresh lemongrass, kaffir lime leaves, and curry leaves, store them in airtight bags in the freezer for up to six months.

BIRDSEYE CHILIES
Fresh chilies freeze well. Place them in an airtight bag in the freezer. They will last for up to six months.

THAWED SPICES
Spices that have been frozen may be slightly limp when they have thawed, but their flavor is not impaired.

SPICE PROFILES

11 COOKING WITH SPICES

It is always exciting to cook with spices – to discover new tastes and sensations, and experiment with unfamiliar combinations and recipes. These Spice Profiles (*Tips* 12–60) illustrate spices in their various forms, describe their aromas and tastes, and suggest which foods combine well with each particular spice.

12 DILL

The leaves and seeds of dill are popular in cooking, mainly in the Northern Hemisphere. Dill is also thought to aid digestion.
- **Aroma & taste:** Warm, pungent, slightly sharp, with a hint of anise. Resembles caraway in aroma.
- **Culinary uses:** Soups, stews, fish and seafood dishes, vinegars, pickles, salads, breads, potatoes, cakes, pastries.

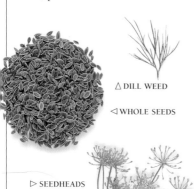

△ DILL WEED

◁ WHOLE SEEDS

▷ SEEDHEADS

13 CELERY

Well known as a vegetable, the seeds and leaves of celery are also delicious as a flavoring.
- **Aroma & taste:** Warm and bitter, with a hint of nutmeg and parsley.
- **Culinary uses:** Soups, stews, sauces, salad dressings, fish and egg dishes.

▷ LEAVES & STALK

△ WHOLE SEEDS

CELERY SALT
A salt-based seasoning, celery salt is easier to obtain than celery seeds but can quickly become stale.

✳ SPICE PROFILES

14 MUSTARD

There are various forms of mustard seeds: black, white, and brown. Brown are the most widely available and most commonly used.

- **Aroma & taste:** Slightly bitter, then hot and aromatic.
- **Culinary uses:** Indian cooking, mustard blends.

WHOLE BROWN SEEDS

15 MUSTARD PRODUCTS

Mustard oil is used in India for deep-frying and stir-frying, and flavors many pickles. Mustard fruits, or *mostarda di Cremona*, make a spicy, unusual accompaniment to cold meats. The fruits are cooked in syrup, which is then reduced and flavored with mustard.

MUSTARD FRUITS

16 PREPARED MUSTARDS

The original prepared mustards were made at home from seeds pounded together with vinegar. Today, there is a great range of commercially prepared mustards. They may be smooth or grainy, and mild or fiery. They are always highly flavored, often with other spices or herbs, and sometimes with other ingredients such as honey or wine.

▷ *German mustard has a sweet flavor and is good with cheese, sausages, and cold meats. You can also use it in cooking.*

△ *American mustard is very mild. Serve it with burgers, steaks, and in sandwiches.*

◁ **Provençal mustard** contains garlic, red peppers, and wine. Try it with grilled meats and in marinades.

▽ **Dijon mustard** is smooth and clean-tasting. It is excellent in salad dressings and sauces for vegetables, meat, and fish.

△ **French coarse-ground mustard** adds crunchiness to sauces and dressings.

△ **Wholegrain mustard** is mild and crunchy. This recipe contains red wine vinegar and cinnamon. It goes well with meat.

▷ **Herb & tomato mustard**, flavored with garlic, suits barbecued and broiled meats.

◁ **English mustard**, made by mixing powder with water, is a hot blend. It is an ideal complement to cold meats and sausages.

15

Hot seeds are often removed before cooking

Ribs contain capsaicin, the source of heat

Outer skin may be removed

17 CHILIES

With about 200 varieties throughout the world, chilies vary greatly in shape, size, color, and heat. They are used fresh or dried.

- **Aroma & taste:** Little aroma, but taste varies from mild to fiery hot.
- **Culinary uses:** Savory dishes, sauces.

◁ PARTS OF A CHILI
The hottest parts of a chili are the seeds and ribs; remove them to reduce fire. The flavor is found inside the flesh.

> **RULE OF THUMB**
> *As a general rule, large, round, fleshy chilies are milder than small, thin-skinned, pointed kinds.*

18 FRESH CHILIES

Fresh chilies are preferred in Thai and Indonesian cooking. Cuisines of Central and South America, and the Caribbean, call for fresh or dried, depending on the dish. Buy fresh chilies that are crisp and smooth. You may need to remove the skins by charring the chilies before cooking. Like other fruits of the genus *Capsicum*, fresh chilies are rich in vitamin C.

△ *Cayenne chilies are widely available. They are long, thin, and very hot.*

▽ *Habanero chilies, from the Caribbean, are blisteringly hot.*

△ *Jalapeños are well-known, moderately hot chilies from Mexico.*

△ *Serrano chilies are green and pungent, and are commonly used in Mexican cooking.*

▷ *Red & green chilies are widely available; some are very pungent.*

19 DRIED CHILIES

A whole range of chilies is available dried; in some dishes, particularly in Spanish cooking, these are preferable to fresh ones. If stored in an airtight jar or plastic box, they will last for a year or more. In many cuisines, dried chilies are toasted briefly, then soaked and ground with other ingredients for a sauce.

△ *Morron chilies*, popular in Spain, have a mildly piquant, smoky taste.

△ *Ancho chilies*, the most commonly used dried chilies in Mexico, are dried poblano chilies.

◁ *Birdseye chilies* are tiny, pointed chilies, usually no more than ¾in (2cm) long. Their use is widespread, and they are extremely hot.

20 CHILI PRODUCTS

Ripe chilies may be ground, dried, crushed, or flaked, and form the basis of many products. True chili powder is made from ground dried chilies. Don't confuse it with the less pungent mix of chilies and other spices and herbs often used to season chili con carne.

◁ *Ground cayenne* consists of small, pungent chilies ground to a powder.

▷ *Chili powder* contains pure chilies (red mix) or a blend of seasonings (dark mix).

△ *Chili flakes* are dried, crushed chilies. They are used in dishes where extra texture is important.

▷ *Tabasco sauce* is one of many chili sauces found worldwide. It adds a fiery zest to savory dishes.

21 USING CHILIES SAFELY

Chilies can cause intense irritation to the skin, eyes, mouth, stomach, and intestines. To be safe, follow these guidelines:

- Use rubber gloves when handling chilies.
- To reduce their heat, remove the seeds and ribs. For dried chilies, cut off the stalk end and shake out the seeds. (*For fresh chilies, see right.*)
- Wash down the work surface well after use.
- Soothe a sore mouth with plain rice, bread, or milk. Do not drink water: it will make it worse.

SEEDING A FRESH CHILI
Cut it in half. Scrape out the seeds with a spoon or knife. Rinse chili, pat dry.

22 MAKING CHILI OIL

Spice-infused oils lend an intriguing flavor to foods and are simple to make. Here, olive oil and dried red chilies are used, but you could try any oil and fewer or more chilies to taste. Drizzle the oil over pizza or pasta, or brush it over grilled meats before serving.

1 △ Heat 1 cup (250ml) oil and 6 tbsp chopped chilies for 10 minutes.

WARNING
Keep the heat very low. If the chilies become too hot, they will give off throat-burning fumes.

2 △ Allow to cool. Add 2 tsp cayenne and 1–2 tbsp Oriental sesame oil. Cover. Leave for 12 hours.

3 ▷ Strain through a lined funnel into a sterilized bottle. Add 2–3 whole chilies for decoration. Store the bottle at room temperature.

23 CHILIES AS A GARNISH

The presentation of spicy dishes can be enhanced by a colorful chili flower.

▪ Using a sharp knife, make several lengthwise slits through a chili from below the stalk to the pointed end. Soak the chili in a bowl of ice water until the ends curl out to form a flower, about 30 minutes. Remove from the water, and pat dry before use.

▪ Wear rubber gloves, or wash your hands immediately after handling the chili.

CHILI FLOWER

24 PAPRIKA

Sweet red peppers are dried and ground to make paprika, essential in Hungarian and Spanish cuisine. The peppers are sweet or hot, so paprika varies in pungency.

▪ **Aroma & taste:** Sweet or lightly pungent, then faintly bitter.

▪ **Culinary uses:** Goulash, poultry and fish dishes, vegetables.

◁ **FRESH RED PEPPER**
The sweet peppers that are dried to make paprika are broad and fleshy. The powder gives food a deep red color.

▷ HUNGARIAN PAPRIKA

25 CARAWAY

Popular in central European and Jewish cooking, caraway seeds are generally used whole, or occasionally ground. Caraway is easily confused with cumin.

▪ **Aroma & taste:** Pungent, warm, and slightly bitter.

▪ **Culinary uses:** Breads, cheeses, sausages, cabbage, soups.

◁ WHOLE SEEDS

▷ **CARAWAY BREAD**
In Germany and Holland, rye breads often contain whole caraway seeds.

26 CASSIA

One of the most ancient of all spices, cassia is essential in Chinese cuisine. Cassia, like cinnamon, is the dried bark of a tree of the laurel family. It is sometimes used instead of cinnamon, although it has a less delicate flavor.

△ DRIED BARK

- **Aroma & taste:** Slightly sweet with a bitter, astringent edge.
- **Culinary uses:** Sauces, braised dishes, curries, pilafs, grains, stewed fruits, chocolate.

◁ GROUND

△ WHOLE BUDS

27 CINNAMON

Like cassia, cinnamon is the dried bark of a tree of the laurel family. Much of the cinnamon sold in North America is actually cassia. The quills are rolled-up pieces of bark. Quillings are broken quills.

- **Aroma & taste:** Sweet, warm, and fragrant.
- **Culinary uses:** Lamb stews, rice dishes, mulled wine, breads, fruit, cakes, desserts, puddings.

▷ QUILLINGS

▽ GROUND

▷ QUILLS

28 KAFFIR LIME

The delicate flavor of kaffir lime enhances many Thai and Indonesian dishes. Use fresh leaves if available. The bitter zest of the fruit may also be used.

- **Aroma & taste:** Clean, floral aroma, similar to lemon verbena.
- **Culinary uses:** Chicken and fish dishes.

△ FRUIT

▷ DRIED LEAVES

◁ FRESH LEAVES

29 CORIANDER & CILANTRO

Both of these are used in cooking worldwide. The seeds (coriander) and leaves (cilantro) are entirely different in smell, taste, and character. The root is also sometimes used. Indian seeds are sweeter than Moroccan ones but are less easy to find.

- **Aroma & taste (seeds):** Sweet, woody, peppery.
- **Culinary uses (seeds):** Meat dishes, vegetables, pickles, baking, chocolate.

◁ WHOLE CORIANDER (MOROCCAN)

△ GROUND (INDIAN)

◁ ROOT

▷ GROUND (MOROCCAN)

▷ *Cilantro has an earthy, citrussy taste.*

▷ WHOLE CORIANDER (INDIAN)

30 SAFFRON

The wiry threads of saffron – the most expensive spice in the world – are the stigmas of the saffron crocus. It takes over 20,000 crocuses to produce just 4oz (125g): every single stigma needs to be hand-picked, and then dried. Saffron threads are preferable to ground saffron, since ground may be adulterated.

△ THREADS

- **Aroma & taste:** Distinctive, fairly bitter aroma and a penetrating, highly aromatic taste.
- **Culinary uses:** Soups, sauces, fish and rice dishes, cakes, breads.

SAFFLOWER
A cheap substitute for saffron, safflower is often wrongly sold as saffron. Safflower is less vibrant than saffron and will color food but not flavor it.

◁ GROUND

31 HOW TO USE SAFFRON

A small amount of saffron is all that is needed to infuse dishes with its distinctive flavor and brilliant gold color. To ensure that the color is evenly distributed, soak the threads in hot water briefly and add them to the dish. Add ground saffron directly to the pan, mixing it in very thoroughly with the other ingredients for even color throughout.

△ SAFFRON THREADS
The threads are red-orange and about 1in (2.5cm) long. The deeper the color, the better the quality.

△ SOAKING SAFFRON
Soak the threads in a little hot water, then add saffron and its liquid to the dish.

32 CUMIN

▷ GROUND

A vast range of Indian, Middle Eastern, North African, American, and Mexican dishes contain cumin. In India, cumin is dry-roasted before use to bring out its flavor.

- **Aroma & taste:** Pungent, slightly bitter, and warm.
- **Culinary uses:** Meat dishes, vegetables, pickles, relishes, salads.

◁ WHOLE SEEDS

> **A NOTE ABOUT AJOWAN**
> *Related to cumin and caraway, ajowan is an Indian spice with a taste similar to thyme. The seeds are used in curries, fish dishes, breads, pickles, and snacks.*

33 TURMERIC

A relative of ginger, turmeric imparts a musky flavor and rich, golden color to Asian dishes. It is mostly sold ground, but the fresh root is occasionally found in the West.

- **Aroma & taste:** Pungent, bitter, and musky.
- **Culinary uses:** Curry powder, vegetable dishes, bean dishes, lentil dishes.

▷ FRESH RHIZOME

▽ GROUND

△ TURMERIC DYE
Turmeric has long been used as a yellow textile dye in Asia. In cooking, it is sometimes used instead of saffron for its color.

34 LEMONGRASS

Common in Southeast Asian cooking, fresh lemongrass is now frequently available in supermarkets in the West. The fresh stalks have more flavor than the dried and the powder. Avoid chewing lemongrass – it is very fibrous.

▪ **Aroma & taste:** Smells and tastes of lemon zest, with a clean, refreshing flavor.

▪ **Culinary uses:** Soups, stews, fish and shellfish dishes, and chicken, beef, and pork dishes.

△ GROUND

△ FRESH STALKS

▷ DRIED STRIPS

35 HOW TO USE LEMONGRASS

Remove the outer leaves of fresh lemongrass stalks and use only the white lower part. Add the stalks to dishes whole (remove before serving), finely sliced, or pounded to a paste with other ingredients. Dried strips must be soaked in water before using.

◁ **PREPARING STALKS**
Use only the lower 4–6in (10–15cm). Bruise the fresh stalk with the flat of a knife to release the flavor. Cut it into small pieces.

▷ CHOPPED STALKS

36 CARDAMOM

After saffron and vanilla, cardamom is the third most costly spice. The flavor is within the seeds – the pod itself is inedible.

- **Aroma & taste:** Mellow aroma and a bitter, strong, warm flavor.
- **Culinary uses:** Garam masala, curry powder, pastries, puddings, ice creams, cakes, breads, coffee.

△ WHITE PODS

▽ GREEN PODS △ GROUND

VARIATIONS
White pods are the same as green but have been bleached. Brown pods (not shown here) are not true cardamom. They are coarser in texture and taste.

37 CLOVES

Whole cloves are the unopened flower buds of a small tree. Ground cloves are a main ingredient of garam masala (*Tip 75*).

- **Aroma & taste:** Assertive, rich, dark aroma. Sharp and bitter before cooking, then a warm flavor.
- **Culinary uses:** Savory dishes, especially ham, and sweet foods.

△ WHOLE BUDS

▷ **INFUSER**
A clove infuser is used in cooking to give the flavor of whole cloves without the texture.

▽ GROUND

△ BLOCK

▷ GROUND

38 ASAFETIDA

Popular in Indian cooking, asafetida is a dried, resinlike substance from the rhizomes of several species of giant fennel. It is very potent, so use sparingly.
- **Aroma & taste:** Extremely strong, unpleasant smell. Bitter, acrid taste before cooking but gives onion flavor when fried.
- **Culinary uses:** Vegetables, legumes, pickles, sauces.

39 USING FRESH ASAFETIDA

Fresh asafetida is best ground before use. Break off small pieces of the block and grind with an absorbent powder, such as rice flour, using a pestle in a mortar. Pieces of fresh asafetida are sometimes rubbed on the grill before cooking meat.

40 FENNEL

Fennel is a truly international spice, used in cooking throughout the world. It is also thought to have strong medicinal properties. Buy whole fennel seeds and grind them as required.
- **Aroma & taste:** Warm and aromatic. Similar to anise, but not as sweet.
- **Culinary uses:** Pork and fish dishes, vegetables, bread, pickles.

◁ SEEDHEADS

▷ WHOLE

AFTER-DINNER REFRESHMENT
Indians serve fennel seeds, sometimes dry-roasted or candied, as a digestive and breath freshener after meals.

41 STAR ANISE

A distinctive flavor in Chinese and Vietnamese cooking, star anise is the fruit of a tree of the magnolia family. Use the fruit whole or broken, or grind as required.

- **Aroma & taste:** Similar to anise and fennel, but more licorice-like, with a sweet note.
- **Culinary uses:** Poultry and pork dishes, braised fish dishes, Asian beef soups.

△ BROKEN FRUIT

FIVE-SPICE POWDER
One of the few spices used in Chinese cooking, star anise is the main flavor of five-spice powder (Tip 65).

△ WHOLE FRUIT

42 JUNIPER

Scandinavia, northern France, Germany, and Alsace use juniper in cooking, but English-speaking countries seldom cook with it, knowing it mainly for its distinctive flavor in gin.

- **Aroma & taste:** Bittersweet, with a hint of pine and turpentine.
- **Culinary uses:** Marinades for beef and pork, pâtés, potatoes, sauerkraut, game.

◁ BERRIES ON PLANT

△ WHOLE BERRIES

△ CRUSHED BERRIES

27

43 GALANGAL

There are two types of galangal: greater and lesser. Both are widely used in Southeast Asia. Outside Asia, lesser galangal is difficult to obtain and is usually dried and sliced. To prepare fresh galangal, see Tip 60, How to prepare fresh ginger.

- **Aroma & taste:** Resembles ginger, with a hint of pepper, eucalyptus, and lemon.
- **Culinary uses:** Soups, stews, curries, Thai curry pastes.

△ FRESH RHIZOME (GREATER GALANGAL)

△ DRIED SLICES (LESSER GALANGAL)

▷ GROUND

▷ FRESH SLICES (GREATER GALANGAL)

44 CURRY LEAVES

These small leaves are used extensively in Indian cooking. They come from a species of small tree that grows throughout the Indian subcontinent and Sri Lanka. They are available in some Asian shops in the West. Buy fresh leaves, if possible: they have much more flavor than dried ones.

- **Aroma & taste:** Currylike smell and flavor, with a citrus note.
- **Culinary uses:** Curries, vegetable dishes.

◁ FRESH LEAVES

▷ DRIED LEAVES

45 NUTMEG & MACE

Unique among spice plants, *Myristica fragrans* produces two distinct spices. Nutmeg is the kernel of the seed. Mace is the lacy growth, or aril, that surrounds the seed.

- **Aroma & taste:** Rich, fresh, warm, and highly aromatic. Nutmeg is sweeter and less refined than mace.
- **Culinary uses:** Clear soups, lamb and veal dishes, vegetables, egg and cheese dishes, milk-based sauces, cakes, fruit desserts, punches.

FOOD OF LOVE
Nutmeg and mace have been highly valued traditionally for their aphrodisiac properties.

▽ NUTMEG GRINDER
This grinder works on the same principle as a pepper mill, and doubles as a store for nutmegs.

△ NUTMEG & MACE

△ MACE BLADES

△ GROUND MACE

◁ GROUND NUTMEG

▽ NUTMEG

◁ NUTMEG GRATER
Traditional graters have a compartment for nutmegs. Many old graters were made as decorative objects of silver, wood, or bone.

46 SPICED VINEGAR
Makes 24 cups (5 liters)

Ingredients
*24 cups (5 liters) white
or red wine vinegar
1 nutmeg
1 small piece of fresh
  ginger, peeled
½ tsp whole cloves
1 tbsp each of mustard
seeds & black peppercorns
¼ cup (50g) salt
zest of ½ orange
6 shallots, quartered*

1 Combine all the
ingredients in a non-
metallic bowl. Cover tightly
and let steep in a warm place
for 3–4 weeks.
2 Strain and pour the liquid through
a funnel into sterilized bottles. Cork.

FLAVORINGS FOR SPICED VINEGAR

47 NIGELLA
The plant that bears nigella seeds,
a popular flavoring in Indian and Middle-
eastern cooking, is a close relative of the
garden plant, Love-in-a-mist. Nigella is also
known as *kalonji* (black onion seeds). It is
usually dry-roasted before cooking.

△ GROUND

▽ WHOLE SEEDS

- **Aroma & taste:** Mild, nutty,
  and acrid. Tastes like a mixture
  of poppy seeds and pepper, and
  is reminiscent of oregano.
- **Culinary uses:** Vegetables,
  legumes, breads.

△ BLUE-GRAY SEEDS

48 POPPY

Poppy seeds enhance both savory and sweet dishes. They may be blue-gray (common in Europe), yellow (India), or brown (Turkey). Unlike the pods, the seeds are not narcotic.

- **Aroma & taste:** Nutty and slightly sweet.
- **Culinary uses:** Breads, cakes, pastries, desserts, as a thickening agent (yellow seeds).

△ BROWN SEEDS   △ YELLOW SEEDS   ▷ SEEDHEAD

49 ALLSPICE

Sometimes known as Jamaica pepper, the allspice berry is widely used in the Caribbean. Elsewhere, it is used mainly in the food industry – in ketchups, pickles, and sausages. Buy it whole and grind as needed.

- **Aroma & taste:** Fragrant and pungent. Taste resembles a peppery mixture of cloves, cinnamon, and nutmeg or mace.
- **Culinary uses:** Soups, stews, curries, cakes, jams, fruit pies.

△ WHOLE BERRIES

▷ GROUND

USING ALLSPICE
For variety, mix black peppercorns and all-spice in a pepper mill and grind over foods.

50 ANISE

Also known as aniseed, anise is related botanically to dill, fennel, cumin, and caraway. It is used primarily in sweet dishes in Europe and in savory ones in India. It is also popular as a digestive.

- **Aroma & taste:** Sweet and distinctly licorice-like.
- **Culinary uses:** Soups, stews, cookies, cakes, breads.

◁ WHOLE SEEDS

▷ GROUND

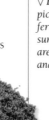

◁ APERITIF
Anise-flavored aperitifs and liqueurs, made with oil extracted from aniseed, are popular in the Mediterranean.

51 PEPPER

Once so highly valued that it was worth its weight in gold, pepper is now the most widely used spice in the West. Black, white, and green peppercorns are all berries from the same vine picked at different stages of maturity. Long pepper is from a related plant.

- **Aroma & taste:** Warm, pungent.
- **Culinary uses:** Stocks, marinades, spice blends, fruit (especially strawberries), as a table condiment.

▽ **Black peppercorns** have been picked when green, left to ferment, and are then sun-dried. They are wrinkled and hard.

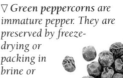

▽ **Green peppercorns** are immature pepper. They are preserved by freeze-drying or packing in brine or vinegar.

◁ **Fresh green berries** have a lively, clean taste, and are not as hot as white or black ones.

▷ **White peppercorns** are ripe berries that have been soaked, skinned, and dried.

◁ **Ground white pepper** is hotter and less subtle than black. In creamy white sauces, it is more attractive than specks of black pepper.

▽ **Ground black pepper** quickly loses its flavor, so grind whole peppercorns as required.

△ **Mixed peppercorns** are a combination of black, green, white, and pink peppercorns.

▷ **Long pepper** is catkinlike and about 1in (2.5cm) long. It is used in the Far East, always whole, in cooking, pickles, and preserves.

SPICE PROFILES

52 CUBEB

Cubebs are the unripe fruits of a plant in the pepper family, but they are closer to allspice in flavor. They are used mainly in Far Eastern and African cooking.

- **Aroma & taste:** Warm, aromatic, with a slightly bitter taste.
- **Culinary uses:** Ras el hanout (*Tip 79*), vegetable dishes, meat stews.

WHOLE BERRIES

53 SUMAC

Widely used in the Middle East, sumac is little known in the West. If you can find the whole berries, crack and soak them in water for 20 minutes, then use the berries and their juice in cooking.

- **Aroma & taste:** Sour and astringent, but not sharp.
- **Culinary uses:** Fish and chicken dishes, salads, kebabs, lentil dishes.

▷ WHOLE BERRIES

◁ GROUND

54 SESAME

Grown for its oil-producing seeds, sesame is used around the world. Its flavor is enhanced by dry-roasting. The black seeds have a particularly strong, earthy flavor.

- **Aroma & taste:** No aroma, but a sweet, nutty taste.
- **Culinary uses:** Rice, dressings, breads, cakes, halva (a sweetmeat).

▷ TAHINI
Made from ground sesame seeds, this paste is delicious in dressings to flavor vegetable and fruit dishes.

55 TAMARIND

Also known as Indian date, this bean-shaped pod is used in the West Indies, India, and Southeast Asia. It adds a pleasantly sour note to cooked dishes.

- **Aroma & taste:** Slightly sweet aroma and a sour, fruity flavor.
- **Culinary uses:** Soups, curries, fish and poultry dishes, lentil and rice dishes, chutneys, cooling drinks, desserts.

◁ WHITE SEEDS

◁ BROWN SEEDS

▷ BLACK SEEDS

▷ ORIENTAL SESAME OIL

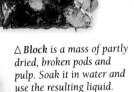

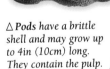

△ **Pulp** is a brown and fleshy mass within the pods. It can contain up to ten seeds.

△ **Block** is a mass of partly dried, broken pods and pulp. Soak it in water and use the resulting liquid.

△ **Pods** have a brittle shell and may grow up to 4in (10cm) long. They contain the pulp.

◁ **Concentrate** is a thick, dark, molasses-like paste with a sharp, acidic taste.

▷ **Slices** are dried pieces of tamarind; soak them in water to bring out the flavor.

35

56 FENUGREEK

In India and the Middle East, fenugreek seeds and leaves are popular flavorings. Dry-roast the seeds to mellow the flavor.

- **Aroma & taste:** Strong, aromatic, bitter.
- **Culinary uses:** Curry powder, pickles, vegetables.

△ GROUND

▽ WHOLE SEEDS

◁ DRIED LEAVES

57 VANILLA

The second most expensive spice in the world, vanilla enhances numerous sweet dishes.
- **Aroma & taste:** Rich, mellow aroma and a fragrant, sweet flavor.
- **Culinary uses:** Ice creams, custard, cakes, puddings, chocolate.

▷ SEEDS

STORING VANILLA PODS
Vanilla pods can be used over and over again, even if they have been infusing milk or a sauce. Keep a pod in a jar of sugar; it flavors the sugar and lasts for years.

△ WHOLE POD

ABOUT SANSHO
One of the few spices used in Japan, sansho is closely related to Sichuan pepper. The berries are ground and are added during cooking or sprinkled on food.

WHOLE BERRIES

58 SICHUAN PEPPER

Also known as fagara, Sichuan pepper is not at all related to black and white pepper. It is a popular table condiment in China and is also used whole, crushed, or ground in cooking. Dry-roast the berries before use.

- **Aroma & taste:** Spicy-woody aroma and a numbing taste.
- **Culinary uses:** Five-spice powder (*Tip 65*), poultry, meat.

59 GINGER

A staple throughout Asia since ancient times, ginger was one of the first Asian spices to be introduced to the rest of the world. Most Asian countries use fresh ginger, often with garlic. In Indian, Arab, and much Western cooking, it is also used dried.

- **Aroma & taste:** Warm aroma with a fresh, woody note. Hot, biting flavor.
- **Culinary uses:** Curry powder, meat and fish dishes, vegetables, pickles, cookies, cakes, puddings, drinks.

△ *Preserved ginger, or stem ginger, consists of pieces of tender ginger steeped in syrup.*

◁ *Dried ginger is occasionally used instead of fresh ginger. Bruise the pieces before use.*

◁ *Ground ginger is used in Europe in baking, and in Asian spice blends.*

▷ *Fresh ginger is a knobby rhizome used in Asian cooking.*

60 HOW TO PREPARE FRESH GINGER

When buying fresh ginger, choose rhizomes that feel firm. The pale yellow flesh should be not too fibrous. The instructions below for preparing fresh ginger also apply to fresh galangal (*Tip 43*).

1 With a sharp chef's knife or cleaver, trim off any awkward-shaped knobs on the ginger.

2 Carefully remove the skin with a knife or vegetable peeler, or scrape it off using a cleaver.

3 Thinly slice the ginger across the grain, crush the slice with the flat of a knife, then dice finely.

FAR EAST

61 THAI SHRIMP SOUP WITH LEMONGRASS
Serves 4

Ingredients
3 stalks lemongrass
7 cups (1.5 liters) fish
or chicken stock
2 fresh green chilies,
seeded & sliced
zest of 1 lime
1lb (500g) large cooked
shrimp, shelled
juice of 2 limes
4 scallions, sliced
1 small fresh red chili,
seeded & sliced
3 tbsp coarsely
chopped cilantro,
to garnish

1 Bruise the lemongrass. Put it in a large saucepan with the stock, green chilies, and lime zest and bring to a boil. Cover and simmer for 20 minutes, then strain.

2 Return the strained stock to the pan, add the shrimp, and simmer for 3–4 minutes. Stir in the lime juice and remove from the heat. Add the scallions and red chili.

USING STOCK
Choose homemade stock always for preference. Good-quality fresh stock is available from large supermarkets (look for it in the chilled cabinets).

TO SERVE
Garnish the soup with chopped cilantro and serve while it is still piping hot.

62 SEVEN-SPICE POWDER

Keeps for 3–4 months in an airtight container

Ingredients

2 tsp white sesame seeds
3 tsp sansho (Tip 58)
1 tsp nori seaweed
*3 tsp flaked dried
tangerine peel*
3 tsp chili powder
1 tsp black sesame seeds
1 tsp poppy seeds

1 Coarsely grind together the white sesame seeds and sansho.
2 Add the nori seaweed and dried tangerine peel and grind again briefly.
3 Stir in the remaining spices and blend well.
■ Seven-spice powder, also known as shichimi togarashi, is a Japanese spice mixture used both in cooking and as a table condiment.

63 CHICKEN WITH NOODLES

Serves 4

Ingredients

*12oz (350g) udon or other
wheat noodles*
*12oz (350g) chicken,
skinned & boned*
6 scallions
*3¹/₂ cups (750ml) dashi
or chicken stock*
4 tbsp light soy sauce
*2 tbsp mirin (available
from Asian stores)*
*Seven-spice powder
(Tip 62), to serve*

1 Boil the noodles in a saucepan until tender. Drain and rinse under cold running water.
2 Cut the chicken into small pieces. Chop the scallions, including the green part, into ¹/₂in (1.5cm) lengths.
3 Combine the dashi, soy sauce, and mirin in a pan and bring to a boil. Add the chicken and simmer for 5–6 minutes. Stir in the scallions and simmer for 1 minute.
4 Reheat the noodles by pouring boiling water over them. Divide between 4 large, warmed bowls. Ladle in the stock and arrange the chicken and scallions on top. Sprinkle seven-spice powder over the top of each serving.

64 SEA BASS WITH STAR ANISE
Serves 4

Ingredients

*1 sea bass, weighing about
3lb (1.5kg), cleaned*
*1 tbsp chopped fresh
ginger*
*2 tbsp Chinese rice wine
or dry sherry*
*2 tsp Five-spice powder
(Tip 65)*
4 star anise
4 scallions, finely chopped
1 tbsp light soy sauce
*2 tsp Oriental sesame oil
salt, to taste*
*finely sliced scallions, to
garnish*

1 Make 2 deep diagonal slashes in each side of the sea bass, using a sharp knife.
2 Mix together the ginger, rice wine, and five-spice powder, then pour the mixture over the fish. Rub it in thoroughly. Let marinate in a cool place for approximately 1 hour.
3 Preheat oven to 400°F/200°C. Combine the star anise, scallions, soy sauce, and sesame oil with a little salt. Stuff the mixture into the cavity of the fish.
4 Carefully wrap the fish in a large piece of oiled foil, making sure it is well sealed. Bake in the oven for 25–35 minutes.

TO SERVE
Carefully slide the fish onto a large serving platter and garnish with finely sliced scallions.

65 FIVE-SPICE POWDER
Keeps for 3–4 months in an airtight container

Ingredients
1 tbsp star anise
1 tbsp Sichuan pepper
*2in (5cm) piece of cassia
or cinnamon*
1 tbsp fennel seeds
½ tbsp whole cloves

Grind all the ingredients to a powder, preferably in an electric grinder.
▪ Five-spice powder is one of the best-known Chinese spice blends. It is used in southern China and Vietnam as a seasoning for roast meat and poultry, and to flavor marinades. Sometimes cardamom, dried ginger, or licorice root are added. Use the powder sparingly.

66 THAI RED CURRY PASTE
Keeps for about 1 month in the refrigerator

Ingredients
3 shallots
3 garlic cloves
2 stalks lemongrass
1 tbsp coriander
1 tsp cumin seeds
1 tsp black peppercorns
10 dried red chilies
*1 tbsp chopped cilantro
root*
1 tbsp ground galangal
2 tsp grated lime zest
*1 small piece of trassi
(available from Asian
stores)*
salt, to taste

1 Chop the shallots, garlic, and lemongrass.
2 Heat a heavy skillet. After 2–3 minutes, add the coriander and cumin seeds and dry-roast until they darken, but do not allow them to burn. Let cool, then grind to a powder together with the peppercorns.
3 Remove the seeds from the chilies and chop the pods. Pound or process all the ingredients to a smooth paste.
▪ Thai red curry paste is a very hot spice mixture used for beef and other robust dishes.

GREEN CURRY PASTE
For green curry paste, follow the recipe for Thai red curry paste, using fresh green chilies instead of dried red ones and adding 2 tbsp chopped cilantro.

67 BEEF CURRY
Serves 6–8

Ingredients
3–4 tbsp Thai red curry paste (Tip 66)
7 cups (1.5 liters) canned coconut milk
4 bay leaves
3lb (1.5kg) beef chuck steak
salt, to taste
chili flowers (Tip 23), to garnish
boiled long-grain white rice, to serve

2 △ Meanwhile, trim off the fat and sinew from the beef and cut the meat into 2in (5cm) cubes.

1 △ To make the sauce, combine the curry paste and coconut milk in a wok or large saucepan and stir until well mixed. Add the bay leaves and bring to a boil over a high heat. Reduce heat to medium and cook for about 15 minutes, stirring occasionally.

CREAMED COCONUT
You can make up your own coconut milk using creamed coconut. Sold in blocks, it must be dissolved in hot water before use.

3 ◁ Add the beef and a pinch of salt to the curry sauce, stir, and return to a boil over a high heat. Reduce the heat to low and simmer, stirring occasionally, for approximately 2 hours. Do not cover the wok or pan during this time, or the coconut milk will curdle.

4 △ Reduce the heat to very low and continue cooking until the beef is tender, about 1½–2 hours, stirring frequently to prevent the curry from sticking. The sauce should be quite thick and rich, and most of the liquid will have evaporated. Skim off the fat from the surface. Taste for seasoning.

TO SERVE
Serve on a bed of rice on individual plates or in shallow bowls. Decorate each serving with a chili flower.

68 CHICKEN SATAY
Serves 6–8

Ingredients
*2lb (1kg) chicken breasts or thighs, boned
& cubed
1 small piece of fresh ginger, crushed
3 garlic cloves, crushed
1 tbsp ground coriander
½ tsp ground galangal
1 tbsp sunflower or peanut oil
¾ cup (150ml) canned coconut milk
cilantro, to garnish
Peanut sauce (Tip 69), to serve*

1 Blend or process together all the ingredients, except the chicken, until smooth. Coat the chicken thoroughly with the mixture. Let marinate in the refrigerator for at least 2 hours. Meanwhile, soak some wooden skewers in water.
2 Thread the chicken onto the skewers and grill for 6–8 minutes, turning halfway through.

69 PEANUT SAUCE
Keeps for up to 10 days in the refrigerator

Ingredients
*2 tbsp sunflower or peanut oil
½ tsp ground coriander
2 tsp ground cumin
1 tsp ground ginger
a few fresh curry leaves
2lb (1kg) large onions, finely chopped
1 tsp trassi, crumbled (available from
Asian stores) (optional)
1¼ cups (350g) smooth peanut butter
¼ cup (50g) coconut cream
1 tbsp sambal oelek (available from
Asian stores)
1–2 tbsp lime or lemon juice*

1 Heat the oil in a saucepan. Add the dry spices, curry leaves, onions, and trassi, if using. Stir well, put a heat diffuser under the pan, and turn the heat to very low. Add the peanut butter and coconut cream.
2 Cook covered for 30–45 minutes, stirring occasionally. If it starts to stick, add 1–2 tbsp water. The sauce should be thick and smooth.
3 Remove the leaves, add the sambal, and cook for 10–15 minutes more. Take off the heat. Add the lime juice.

TO SERVE
Garnish the chicken satay with cilantro and serve with peanut sauce on the side.

INDIA

70 FRUIT CHAT
Serves 6

Ingredients
3 potatoes, peeled, boiled, & diced
½ cucumber, peeled, seeded, & cubed
2 ripe bananas, sliced
1 ripe papaya, cubed
1 ripe mango, cubed
1 eating apple, cubed
2 slices fresh pineapple, cubed
1 orange, in segments
2 tbsp Chat masala (Tip 71)
juice of 1 lemon
small lettuce leaves, to serve

1 Put all the vegetables and fruit into a bowl. Sprinkle in the chat masala and lemon juice and stir.
2 Arrange 5 or 6 lettuce leaves in a circle on individual plates and add the fruit mixture.

71 CHAT MASALA
Keeps for 3–4 months in an airtight container

Ingredients
1 tsp cumin seeds
1 tsp black peppercorns
½ tsp ajowan seeds (Tip 32)
1 tsp dried pomegranate seeds (optional)
1 tsp black salt (available from Asian stores)
1 tsp coarse salt
large pinch of crushed dried mint leaves
½ tsp cayenne
½ tsp ground ginger
¼ tsp ground asafetida
2 tsp mango powder (available from Asian stores)

1 Grind the cumin, peppercorns, ajowan and pomegranate seeds, if using, and both salts to a powder.
2 Add the mint, cayenne, ginger, asafetida, and mango powder.
▪ Chat masala tastes sour but is delicious with fruit and vegetable salads.

TO SERVE
Present fruit chat as a first course or as an accompaniment.

72 MIXED VEGETABLE CURRY
Serves 6–8

Ingredients
5 tbsp vegetable oil
1 cinnamon stick
6 whole cloves
4 onions, diced
3 garlic cloves
1–2 tbsp Curry powder (Tip 73)
4 potatoes, peeled & diced
4 carrots, chopped
1 cauliflower, divided into florets
1lb (500g) green beans, cut into
2in (5cm) lengths
4 large tomatoes, peeled & chopped
9oz (250g) frozen peas, thawed
salt, to taste
4¼ cups (900ml) canned coconut milk
boiled long-grain white rice, to serve

TO SERVE
*Divide the rice among
individual plates and
spoon the curry beside it.
This dish may be made up to 3
days in advance and refrigerated.
Reheat thoroughly before serving.*

1 Heat the oil in a sauté pan or saucepan. Add the cinnamon and cloves and cook until fragrant. Add the onions and garlic and sauté until just beginning to color. Add the curry powder and cook over a low heat for about 2–3 minutes, stirring constantly.

2 Add the potatoes to the pan with the carrots, cauliflower florets, green beans, tomatoes, peas, and salt. Sauté, stirring occasionally, for approximately 3–5 minutes, until all the vegetables are thoroughly coated with the spice mixture in the pan.

73 CURRY POWDER

Keeps for 3–4 months in an airtight container

Ingredients

6 dried red chilies
1oz (25g) coriander
2 tsp cumin seeds
½ tsp mustard seeds
1 tsp black peppercorns
1 tsp fenugreek seeds
10 fresh curry leaves
½ tsp ground ginger
1 tbsp ground turmeric

1 Remove the seeds from the chilies.
2 Dry-roast the coriander, cumin, mustard seeds, peppercorns, fenugreek, and chilies over medium heat until they darken, stirring or shaking the pan often to prevent burning. Let cool, then grind to a powder.
3 Dry-roast the curry leaves in the pan for a few minutes, then grind and add them to the mixture with the ginger and turmeric. Mix well.
▪ Curry powder comes in many forms. This recipe is for a medium-hot blend to use in any dish that requires curry powder.

3 Add the coconut milk to the vegetables and stir well. Cover the pan and simmer for 15–20 minutes, until the vegetables are tender and the sauce is thick and rich. Remove and discard the cloves and cinnamon stick before serving.

74 LIME PICKLE
Makes about 1¾ cups (300ml)

Ingredients
6 limes
¼ cup (50g) salt
1 tbsp mustard seeds
1 tsp fenugreek seeds
seeds from 2 star anise
4 small fresh green chilies
½ cup (125g) soft brown sugar
1 tbsp ground ginger
3–4 tbsp water

1 Cut the limes into quarters. Place them in a wide, flat bowl and sprinkle the salt over them. Leave until the next day.
2 Heat the mustard and fenugreek seeds, star anise, and chilies in a dry skillet. Cover, since the seeds will sputter. When the sputtering subsides, remove from the heat and set aside.
3 Strain the liquid from the limes into a saucepan. Add the sugar, ginger, and water and boil until the sugar dissolves. Let cool.
4 Put the limes and spices into a sterilized preserving jar. Mix well. Pour the cooled sugar mixture over the limes. Cover and store in a cool place for 4 weeks before using.

75 GARAM MASALA
Keeps for 3–4 months in an airtight container

Ingredients
2 cinnamon sticks
3 dried bay leaves
1½oz (40g) cumin seeds
1oz (25g) coriander
¾oz (20g) cardamom seeds
¾oz (20g) black peppercorns
½oz (15g) whole cloves
½oz (15g) ground mace

1 Break the cinnamon sticks into pieces. Crumble the bay leaves.
2 Place a heavy skillet over a medium heat. After 2–3 minutes, put in the cinnamon, bay leaves, cumin, coriander, cardamom, peppercorns, and cloves. Dry-roast until the color darkens, stirring or shaking the pan frequently to prevent burning. Let cool.
3 Grind the roasted spices and stir in the mace.
▪ Garam masala is a pungent spice mixture from North India. It adds an intriguing flavor to onion-based sauces for meats and poultry. Change the proportions to suit your palate, and use sparingly.

76 AROMATIC COLD CHICKEN
Serves 6

Ingredients

3 tbsp natural yogurt
1 tsp each of Garam masala (Tip 75) & ground turmeric
salt, to taste
6 chicken breasts, skinned & boned
2½ cups (600ml) chicken stock
4 cardamom pods
1 fresh curry or bay leaf
2 tbsp (25g) butter
1 tbsp gram flour (besan) (available in Asian stores)
½ tbsp all-purpose flour
½ tsp ground mace
¼ tsp ground cardamom seeds
4 tbsp heavy cream or thick plain yogurt
mixed salad leaves, to serve

1 Blend together the yogurt, ½ tsp each of garam masala and turmeric, and salt. Rub the mix into the chicken and marinate for 1 hour.
2 Heat the stock with the cardamoms and curry leaf. Put in the chicken breasts and simmer for 15–20 minutes, or until tender.
3 Lift out the chicken and transfer to a serving dish. Cool, then chill. Strain and reserve the stock. Let cool while making the sauce.
4 To make the sauce, melt the butter in a pan and stir in both kinds of flour until smooth. Add the remaining garam masala and turmeric, and a little salt, then whisk in 2½ cups (450ml) of the reserved stock. Bring to a boil and simmer for 15 minutes, stirring from time to time. Stir in the mace, cardamom seeds, and cream. Cool, then chill the sauce.

TO SERVE
Spoon the chilled sauce over the chicken. Serve with mixed salad leaves.

77 SPICY FISH STEW
Serves 6

Ingredients
6 tbsp vegetable oil
3 onions (1 chopped, 2 thinly sliced)
1 apple, peeled & chopped
1 tsp each of ground cumin & coriander
½ tsp each of ground ginger & cloves
¼ tsp cayenne pepper
1½ tbsp cornstarch
1¾ cups (400ml) canned coconut milk
salt & pepper, to taste
2 tbsp paprika
1¼ cups (300ml) fish stock
6 tomatoes, peeled & coarsely chopped
6 cloves garlic, finely chopped
4 bay leaves
2 celery stalks, thinly sliced
2 carrots, thinly sliced
2lb (1kg) monkfish filets or other firm
white fish, cut into strips

2 △ Put the cornstarch in a small bowl. Add 2–3 tbsp of the coconut milk; blend to a smooth paste. Add the remaining coconut milk to the pan with the onion and apple, bring to a boil, and stir in the cornstarch paste; it will thicken at once. Remove the pan from the heat; season. Set aside.

1 ▽ To make the sauce, melt 2 tbsp oil in a saucepan. Add the chopped onion and apple and cook until soft. Add the spices, except the paprika. Cook over a low heat for 2 minutes.

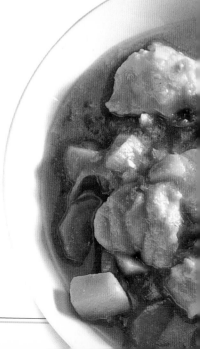

3 △ Heat the remaining oil in a casserole. Add the sliced onions and cook for about 3–5 minutes, until soft but not brown. Add the paprika and cook for about 1 minute, stirring to combine evenly with the onions.

4 △ Add the fish stock, tomatoes, garlic, bay leaves, celery, and carrots to the casserole with a little salt and pepper. Bring the mixture to a boil. Reduce the heat and simmer for about 15–20 minutes, until the liquid is reduced by one-third.

TO SERVE
Ladle the stew into individual warmed bowls and serve hot.

5 △ Stir in the sauce, bring back to a boil, and add the fish. Cover and simmer, stirring occasionally, for about 12–15 minutes, or until the fish flakes easily. Discard the bay leaves and serve.

NORTH AFRICA & MIDDLE EAST

78 HARISSA
Keeps for up to 6 weeks in the refrigerator

Ingredients
2oz (50g) dried red chilies
2 garlic cloves
a pinch of salt
1 tsp caraway seeds
1½ tsp ground cumin
2 tsp coriander
1 tsp crushed dried
mint leaves
olive oil

1 Seed the chilies and tear them into pieces. Soak in warm water until they soften, about 20 minutes. Drain, and pound or process.
2 Crush the garlic with a little salt.
3 Pound, blend, or process all the ingredients to a paste, then stir in 1–2 tbsp of olive oil. Transfer to a jar, cover with a layer of olive oil, and refrigerate until required.
■ Harissa is used in cooking in vegetable or meat stews, or as a table condiment. It is a fiery sauce, so use sparingly at first.

79 RAS EL HANOUT
Make up your own blend to taste

This variable Moroccan blend, which is best ground as needed, is delicious in game dishes, lamb tagines (stews), and couscous and rice stuffings. Ingredients could include: allspice, bay leaves, black pepper, cantharides, cardamom, cassia, chilies, cinnamon, cloves, cubebs, fennel seeds, galangal, ginger, grains of paradise, lavender, long pepper, mace, nigella, nutmeg, orris root, rose buds, and turmeric.

80 HARIRA
Serves 4

Ingredients
6oz (175g) chicken breast, skinned, boned, & chopped
1 onion, chopped
2 garlic cloves, chopped
3 tomatoes, peeled & chopped
7 cups (1.5 liters) chicken stock
1/2 tsp ground cinnamon
1/2 tsp ground cumin
1/2 tsp ground Ras el hanout (Tip 79) (optional)
1/2 tsp ground ginger
salt, to taste
1 cup (125g) cooked chickpeas
1 cup (125g) vermicelli
a handful of chopped cilantro or parsley
2 eggs, lightly beaten
1 tsp Harissa (Tip 78), plus extra to serve (to taste)

PLEASE NOTE
This soup contains eggs that are cooked only until they are just firm.

1 Put the chicken, onion, garlic, and tomatoes in a saucepan with the stock. Bring to a boil and remove any scum. Add the spices and salt, cover the pan, and simmer for about 1 hour.
2 Add the chickpeas and vermicelli and cook for another 10–15 minutes, or until the pasta is cooked. Stir in the cilantro.
3 Take the pan off the heat and stir in the eggs and harissa. Serve with extra harissa if desired.

81 SPICED OLIVES
Makes about 1lb (500g)

Ingredients
1lb (500g) green olives in brine
4–5 garlic cloves
1 tbsp coriander or fennel seeds,
lightly crushed
½ lemon, sliced
1 fresh bay leaf
extra-virgin olive oil

1 Drain and rinse the olives. Crack them by hitting with a rolling pin or mallet, then put them into a large jar interspersed with the garlic, coriander, lemon, and bay leaf.
2 Cover with olive oil and a lid. Store in a cool place or refrigerate for 2–3 weeks before using.

82 FALAFEL
Serves 4

Ingredients
2 cups (250g) chickpeas, soaked for
36 hours, rinsed, & drained
1 large onion, chopped
3 garlic cloves, crushed
a handful of fresh parsley or cilantro,
coarsely chopped
1 tsp each of ground coriander & cumin
¼ tsp cayenne (optional)
salt, to taste
¼ tsp baking powder
1–2 tbsp all-purpose flour, if required
oil for deep-frying
tahini (Tip 54), pita bread, & salad
vegetables, to serve

To Serve
*Serve hot or warm with tahini sauce,
sliced pita bread, and salad vegetables.*

1 Grind the chickpeas to a paste in a food processor. As they crumble, add the onion, garlic, and parsley. Process to a fine paste.
2 Blend in the spices, salt, baking powder, and flour, if required (this will help the falafel adhere). Leave in a cool place for at least 1 hour.
3 Form the mixture into small balls, each the size of a walnut. Flatten them slightly and let rest again for 15 minutes.
4 Deep-fry the falafel for 3–4 minutes, turning once. Drain on paper towels.

83 FISH COUSCOUS
Serves 6

Ingredients
3lb (1.5kg) gray mullet, cod, bream, or other firm white fish, cleaned & cut into large chunks (save heads & trimmings)
6 cups (1.25 liters) water
salt, to taste
pinch of cayenne
1 tbsp sunflower or peanut oil
2 large onions, chopped
2 celery stalks, cut into chunks
3 carrots, cut into chunks
3 small turnips, quartered
1/2 tsp saffron threads
1 1/2 tsp tabil or ground cumin & coriander
3 zucchinis, cut into chunks
1 cup (125g) shredded cabbage
1 cup (125g) frozen peas, thawed
3 tomatoes, skinned & quartered
1lb (500g) couscous
Harissa (Tip 78) or paprika & cayenne, to taste

1 To make the stock, put all the fish and vegetable trimmings in a saucepan with the water, salt, and cayenne. Simmer for 20 minutes, strain, and reserve. (Alternatively, use a fish stock cube.)

2 Heat the oil in a pan and sauté the onions until golden. Add the celery, carrots, turnips, and the stock, then the saffron, tabil, and salt. Cover and simmer for 15 minutes, then add the zucchinis, cabbage, peas, and tomatoes. Add more water to cover the vegetables if necessary. Simmer for 10 minutes more. Put in the fish chunks and simmer for about 10 minutes.

3 Cook the couscous according to package instructions. Turn it out into a large bowl, breaking up lumps with a fork. To make a hot-tasting sauce, take out a ladleful of stock and stir in the harissa.

TO SERVE
Spoon the stew over the couscous and serve with the harissa sauce on the side.

84 MOROCCAN SPICY CHICKEN
Serves 4

Ingredients
a large pinch of saffron threads
3–4 tbsp boiling water
3½lb (1.75kg) chicken, cut up
6 onions (4 sliced, 2 finely chopped)
1lb (500g) tomatoes, seeded & chopped
⅓ cup (75g) chopped dried apricots
2 tbsp clear honey
2 tsp ground cinnamon
1 tsp ground ginger
3 sprigs of fresh parsley, chopped
salt & pepper, to taste
½ cup (125ml) olive oil
Almond couscous
½ cup (50g) slivered almonds
6oz (175g) couscous
2 tbsp (25g) butter, cut into pieces

1 △ Preheat oven to 350°F/180°C. Place the saffron threads in a small bowl and add the boiling water. Set aside. Place the chicken in a tagine or heavy casserole and cover with the sliced onions and tomatoes.

2 △ Mix the chopped onions, saffron and its liquid, dried apricots, honey, cinnamon, ginger, chopped parsley, and salt and pepper together in a bowl. Add the olive oil, then spoon the mixture over the chicken in an even layer.

3 △ Cover tightly and bake for about 1½ hours, until the chicken is tender when tested with a fork.

TO SERVE
Arrange the chicken pieces on warmed plates and serve hot with almond couscous (see below).

△ **FOR THE ALMOND COUSCOUS**
Preheat oven to 350°F/180°C. Lay the almonds on a baking sheet and toast in the oven until browned, about 10–12 minutes. Cook the couscous according to package instructions. While it is still hot, add the butter and almonds. Stir with a fork to remove any lumps. Season to taste.

85 ARAB BREAD
Serves 6

Ingredients
½ packet easy-blend yeast
1 tsp salt
4 cups (500g) white bread flour
1½–2 cups (350–450ml) warm water
1 egg, lightly beaten
1 tbsp poppy, sesame, or nigella seeds

1 Sprinkle the yeast and salt over the flour. Add water gradually, enough to form a fairly stiff dough, then knead until elastic.
2 Place the dough in an oiled bowl and cover with plastic wrap or a cloth. Let rise in a warm place until doubled in bulk, about 1½ hours.
3 Divide the dough in 2 and form into round loaves. Place on an oiled baking sheet, cover, and let rise for 30 minutes. Preheat oven to 400°F/200°C.
4 Brush the tops with egg and sprinkle with one of the spices. Bake for 8–10 minutes, then reduce heat to 325°F/160°C and bake for 15–20 minutes more.

EUROPE

86 MUSSEL SOUP WITH SAFFRON
Serves 6

Ingredients

*2lb (1kg) mussels,
shells on
3 tbsp (40g) butter
1 onion, chopped
2 leeks, thinly sliced
1 carrot, diced
1 cup (125g) diced celeriac
4¼ cups (900ml) water
a few saffron threads
salt & pepper, to taste
mussels in shells & flat-
leaf parsley, to garnish*

1 Scrub the mussels, remove the beards, and discard any that are broken or open. Just cover the bottom of a large pan with water, add the mussels, cover, and cook over a high heat, shaking the pan occasionally, until they open.
2 Discard any mussels that have not opened. Keep a few in their shells for garnish, remove the rest, and set aside. Strain the cooking liquid through muslin and reserve.
3 Melt the butter and sauté the onion, leeks, and carrot for 5 minutes. Add the celeriac and cook gently for 10 minutes. Stir in the reserved liquid and water and simmer for 15 minutes.
4 Soak the saffron in a little hot water and stir into the soup. Season with salt and pepper.
5 Put the mussels into the soup just long enough to heat through. Serve immediately.

TO SERVE
*Garnish with mussels
in their shells and sprigs
of flat-leaf parsley.*

87 COUNTRY TERRINE

Serves 8–10

Ingredients

1 slice cooked ham, about
4oz (125g), cut into long,
⅜in- (1cm-) wide strips
2 tbsp brandy
salt & pepper
1 tbsp (15g) butter
1 onion, finely diced
2 garlic cloves, finely
chopped
3 sprigs of fresh thyme,
chopped
4oz (125g) raw chicken
livers, coarsely chopped
1¼lb (625g) ground pork,
part fat, part lean
8oz (250g) ground veal
¼ tsp ground allspice
a pinch each of ground
nutmeg & cloves
2 eggs, lightly beaten
8oz (250g) barding fat
1 bay leaf
gherkins, small pickled
onions, & thyme sprigs,
to garnish
crusty bread, to serve

TO SERVE
*Garnish with
gherkin fans,
pickled onions, and
thyme sprigs. Serve
with crusty bread.*

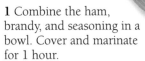

1 Combine the ham,
brandy, and seasoning in a
bowl. Cover and marinate
for 1 hour.
2 Melt the butter in a skillet. Add the onion and
cook until softened and brown. Put into a bowl
and let cool. Add the garlic, thyme, chicken
livers, pork, veal, allspice, nutmeg, and cloves;
season. Add the eggs. Strain in the marinade
from the ham and mix well.
3 Preheat oven to 350°F/180°C.
4 Line the base and sides of a 1¾ pint (1 liter)
terrine with the barding fat, reserving 1 piece.
Spoon in half of the meat mixture, then arrange
the strips of ham on the top. Add the remaining
mixture, fold over the fat overhanging the sides,
then top the terrine with the reserved fat and
the bay leaf. Cover tightly.
5 Set the terrine in a roasting pan half-filled
with water and bring the water to a boil on the
top of the stove. Transfer the terrine in its pan
to the oven and bake for about 1¼–1½ hours.
Remove the terrine from the pan and let it cool
to tepid. Remove the lid, cover the terrine with
a double layer of foil, and set a weight on top.
Refrigerate for about 1 day.
6 Discard any fat from the surface of the terrine.
Cut it into ⅜in (1cm) thick slices and serve.

88 MUSHROOMS À LA GRECQUE
Serves 4

Ingredients
2 tsp each of coriander
& black peppercorns
2 bay leaves
3 sprigs of fresh thyme
2 sprigs of parsley
1 tbsp tomato purée
1½ cups (375ml) water or chicken stock,
plus extra if needed
juice of ½ lemon
2 tbsp dry white wine
1 tbsp vegetable oil
1 tbsp olive oil
12 baby onions
1lb (500g) button mushrooms
1lb (500g) tomatoes, peeled
& coarsely chopped
salt, to taste
thyme sprigs, to garnish

TO SERVE
*This dish is best served at room temperature.
Garnish with a sprig of thyme.*

1 △ To make the spice bag, place the coriander, peppercorns, bay leaves, and thyme and parsley sprigs on a small piece of muslin. Tie them up with string to make a small bag.

2 ▷ To make the cooking liquid, put the tomato purée into a small bowl. Add the water, lemon juice, and wine. Whisk together, then set aside.

3 △ Heat both kinds of oil in a sauté pan or saucepan. Add the onions and sauté until lightly browned, about 3 minutes. Add the mushrooms, the spice bag, and the chopped tomatoes.

4 △ Pour in the cooking liquid – there should be enough almost to cover the vegetables. Add salt to taste. Bring to a boil and boil rapidly, stirring occasionally. Add a little stock or water as the liquid evaporates, if necessary, to prevent the vegetables from sticking. Cook for 25–30 minutes; test to check that the vegetables are tender. Discard the spice bag and let cool.

89 POTATOES WITH JUNIPER

Serves 6

Ingredients
1 tbsp (15g) butter, plus extra for topping
4 shallots, chopped
6oz (175g) smoked bacon, diced
1lb (500g) potatoes, peeled & sliced
salt & pepper
½ tsp juniper berries, crushed
½ cup (150ml) water
flat-leaf parsley, to garnish

1 Melt the butter in a saucepan and cook the shallots slowly until softened. Add the bacon and fry for a few minutes more.
2 Preheat oven to 325°F/160°C. In a casserole, layer the shallot and bacon mixture with the potatoes. Season and add juniper to each layer; finish with the potatoes. Add the water.
3 Cover tightly with foil, then the lid. Bake for 1½–2 hours. Dab with butter and place under the broiler until the top is golden.

90 VENISON WITH GREEN PEPPERCORNS
Serves 4

Ingredients
4 tbsp (50g) butter
8 noisettes of venison,
total weight about 2–2½lb
(1–1.25kg)
4 shallots, finely chopped
2 tbsp brandy
1 tbsp French mustard
1 cup (250ml) beef stock
1 tbsp green peppercorns
½ cup (150ml) crème
fraîche or heavy cream
salt, to taste
flat-leaf parsley, to garnish
steamed zucchini & carrot
ribbons, to serve

1 Melt the butter in a frying pan and sauté the venison for 3–4 minutes each side, or more if necessary, until lightly browned and cooked through. Remove to a serving dish. Keep warm.
2 Add the shallots to the pan and cook for 3–4 minutes. Heat the brandy in a small pan or ladle, then ignite and pour over the shallots.
3 Stir in the mustard, add the stock, and bring to a boil. Boil rapidly to reduce by half, then add the peppercorns, crème fraîche, and salt. Heat through, spoon over the noisettes, and serve.

TO SERVE
Garnish with flat-leaf parsley, and serve with zucchini and carrot ribbons.

91 QUATRE ÉPICES

Keeps for 3–4 months in an airtight container

Ingredients
5 tsp black peppercorns
1 tsp whole cloves
1 tsp ground ginger
2 tsp grated nutmeg

Grind the peppercorns and cloves to a fine powder. Stir in the ginger and nutmeg.
■ Quatre épices (four spices) is a French blend used in charcuterie and in dishes that need long simmering, such as stews.

92 MIXED SPICE

Keeps for 3–4 months in an airtight container

Ingredients
1 small piece of cinnamon
1 tbsp whole cloves
1 tbsp coriander
1 tbsp allspice
1 tbsp ground mace
1 tbsp grated nutmeg

Grind the cinnamon, cloves, coriander, and allspice to a fine powder. Stir in the mace and nutmeg and mix well.
■ Mixed spice, also known as pudding spice, is an English blend of sweet spices, most commonly used in cookies, cakes, and hot puddings.

93 MULLED WINE

Makes about 3 cups (750ml)

Ingredients
½ cup (150ml) water
1 small piece of cinnamon
1 small piece of dried ginger, bruised
8 whole cloves
a few strips of orange zest
⅜ cup (75g) sugar
3 cups (750ml) red wine
cinnamon sticks & orange slices, to decorate

1 Place the water in a large saucepan with the cinnamon, ginger, cloves, orange zest, and sugar. Bring to a boil and simmer to a thick syrup.
2 Pour in the wine and heat to just below the boiling point.
■ Strain or ladle the wine into individual glasses. If you wish, add a cinnamon stick and orange slice to each glass.

94 GINGERBREAD COOKIES
Makes 6–8

Ingredients
¾ cup (150g) clear honey
⅜ cup (75g) soft brown
sugar
2 tbsp (25g) butter
¾ tsp Mixed spice
(Tip 92)
2 tsp ground ginger
a pinch of black pepper
½ tsp ground cardamom
seeds
3 cups (375g) flour
1 egg yolk
1 tsp baking soda
a handful of raisins
(optional)
2oz (50g) confectioners'
sugar, sifted (optional)
1 tsp lemon juice
(optional)

1 Heat the honey, sugar, and butter in a heavy-based saucepan, stirring until the mixture is smooth and the sugar has dissolved. Stir in all the spices and let cool.

2 Sift two-thirds of the flour into a bowl and add the honey mixture and egg yolk. Mix well. Dissolve the baking soda in a spoonful of warm water and add to the mixture. Knead in just enough remaining flour to make a firm dough that comes away from the bowl's sides.

3 Preheat oven to 325°F/160°C. Roll out the dough on a lightly floured surface to about ½in (1cm) thick. Cut out shapes or figures; press in raisins for eyes, if desired. Place on a greased, floured baking sheet. Bake for 10–12 minutes. Cool on a wire rack.

4 If icing the cookies, mix the confectioners' sugar and lemon juice together with 1 tsp warm water. Decorate the cookies when cool.

THE AMERICAS & CARIBBEAN

95 CEVICHE (MARINATED FISH)
Serves 4

Ingredients
6oz (175g) salmon
6oz (175g) brill, turbot, or plaice
6oz (175g) cod filet
juice of 2–3 lemons
1–2 fresh green chilies, seeded & finely chopped
1 small mild onion, finely chopped
½ avocado, peeled, pitted, & cubed
2 tomatoes, peeled, seeded, & chopped
½ cup (125ml) olive oil
handful of cilantro, chopped
salt & pepper, to taste
cilantro & avocado slices, to garnish

1 Remove any skin and bones from the fish and cut the flesh into small cubes. Put the cubes into a nonmetallic dish with the lemon juice, turn to coat all the fish, and let marinate covered in the refrigerator for 5–6 hours.
2 Drain the lemon juice from the fish and combine it with the chilies, onion, avocado, tomatoes, olive oil, and cilantro. Season with salt and pepper and pour over the fish in a serving dish. Chill until ready to serve.

TO SERVE
Serve the fish well chilled. Garnish with cilantro and slices of avocado.

96 MARINATED SHRIMP
Serves 4

Ingredients
½ cup (150ml) olive oil
3 tbsp fresh lime juice
1 tsp Worcestershire sauce
2 tsp Tabasco sauce or other chili
sauce
a pinch of salt
1lb (500g) extra-large shrimp,
cooked & shelled
2 avocados
mixed salad leaves, to serve
lime halves, to garnish

1 In a nonmetallic dish, combine the oil, lime juice, Worcestershire sauce, Tabasco, and salt. Add the shrimp and let marinate in a cool place for about 1 hour.

2 Just before serving, slice the avocados and arrange on individual plates with the salad leaves and shrimp. Pour over a little marinade and garnish with the lime halves.

97 CAJUN SEASONING
Keeps for about 4–6 weeks in the refrigerator

Ingredients
1 large garlic clove
½ small onion
1 tsp paprika
½ tsp ground black pepper
½ tsp ground cumin
½ tsp mustard powder
½ tsp cayenne
1 tsp dried thyme
1 tsp dried oregano
1 tsp salt

1 Crush the garlic and onion with a pestle in a mortar or chop very finely.
2 Combine the remaining ingredients and add them to the garlic and onions. Mix well.
▪ Cajun seasoning is a traditional spicy blend from Louisiana. Rub it into meat or fish before grilling or roasting or add it to gumbos (stews with okra) and jambalayas (rice dishes) for zing.

98 LOUISIANA DIRTY RICE
Serves 4

Ingredients
1–1½ cups (300–350ml) chicken stock
1¼ cups (250g) white long-grain rice
2 tbsp sunflower oil
2 onions, chopped
2 celery stalks, sliced
1 small green pepper, seeded & diced
2 garlic cloves, chopped
1 quantity Cajun seasoning (Tip 97)
10oz (300g) raw chicken livers, diced
chopped flat-leaf parsley plus sprigs, to garnish

1 In a large saucepan, bring 1 cup (300ml) of stock to a boil. Add the rice and bring back to a boil. Cover, place on a very low heat over a heat diffuser, and cook for 15 minutes, until the stock is absorbed. Turn off the heat, leaving the pan covered.

2 While the rice is cooking, heat the oil in a large, heavy saucepan and gently fry the onions, celery, green pepper, and garlic, stirring well.

3 Add the Cajun seasoning and chicken livers and cook over a gentle heat until the livers are browned, about 2–3 minutes, scraping the pan to keep the mixture from sticking. If it becomes too dry, add a little extra stock.

4 Add the rice to the chicken livers and mix well. Cover tightly with a lid. Remove the pan from the heat. Leave it in a warm place for 6–8 minutes so that all the flavors blend.

To Serve
Garnish with flat-leaf parsley and serve warm, not hot.

99 BOLIVIAN CORN PIE
Serves 6

Ingredients
8 ears of corn
⅓ cup (50g) raisins
4 tbsp (50g) butter
salt & pepper
1 tbsp sugar (optional)
5–6 tbsp milk
2 eggs
2 tbsp sunflower oil
2 onions, chopped
3 tomatoes, peeled, seeded, & chopped
1 tsp chopped fresh oregano
1–2 tbsp ground chili
1 tsp ground cumin
½ cup (75–125g) black olives
2lb (1kg) chicken, cooked, skinned, boned, & cut into small pieces
2 hard-boiled eggs, chopped
1 egg white
oregano sprigs, to garnish

1 Grate the corn from the ears. You should have about 1½lb (750g) of kernels. Or, scrape a knife down the sides to remove the kernels, and blend to a mush in a food processor. Soak the raisins in warm water for 10 minutes, then drain.
2 Melt the butter in a saucepan. Add the corn, seasoning, and sugar, if using. Stir in 5 tbsp milk. Beat in the eggs, one at a time, over a very low heat, until thickened. Do not allow to boil. If it seems very thick, add a little more milk.
3 In another saucepan, heat the oil and gently fry the onions until golden. Add the tomatoes, oregano, chili, and cumin; season. Stir in the raisins and olives. Remove from the heat and stir in the chicken and hard-boiled eggs. Mix well.
4 Preheat oven to 400°F/200°C. Place a thin layer of the corn mixture in a greased earthenware or soufflé dish. Cover with the chicken mixture, and top with the remaining corn.
5 With a fork, lightly whisk the egg white; brush it over the top of the corn. Bake the pie for 50 minutes to 1 hour until golden brown.

TO SERVE
Garnish with sprigs of oregano.

100 JAMAICAN JERK SEASONING

Keeps for up to 6 weeks in the refrigerator

Ingredients
3–6 habanero chilies, seeded & sliced
3 scallions, chopped
3 shallots, chopped
3 garlic cloves, chopped
small bunch of chives, chopped
1in (2cm) fresh ginger, chopped
2 tbsp chopped fresh thyme
1 tbsp ground allspice
2 tsp ground black pepper
1½ tsp ground cinnamon
¼ tsp ground cloves
3–4 tbsp sunflower oil

1 Put the chilies, scallions, shallots, garlic, chives, ginger, and thyme into a food processor and purée to a firm paste, scraping down the sides of the bowl.
2 Add the allspice, pepper, cinnamon, cloves, and oil, and blend until you have a thick paste. If necessary, add a little more oil or a tablespoon of water.
■ Jamaican jerk seasoning gives a wonderful flavor to barbecued or broiled fish and meat.

101 JERKED CHICKEN

Serves 6

Ingredients
2lb (1kg) chicken pieces
1 quantity Jamaican jerk seasoning
(Tip 100)
2–3 tbsp sunflower oil

1 Make slits in the meat. Rub the seasoning well into the chicken pieces on all sides and let marinate in the refrigerator for a minimum of 2 hours.
2 Remove the chicken from the refrigerator and bring it to room temperature. Brush lightly with oil and broil or barbecue for about 8–10 minutes, depending on the size and thickness, turning once.

INDEX

A
ajowan, 23
allspice, 31
almond couscous, 57
anise, 32
Arab bread, 57
aromatic cold chicken, 49
asafetida, 26

B
beef curry, 42–3
Bolivian corn pie, 68
bread, Arab, 57
bruising spices, 10
buying spices, 9

C
Cajun seasoning, 66
    Louisiana dirty rice, 67
caraway, 19
cardamom, 25
Caribbean, 65–9
cassia, 20
cayenne, 17
celery, 13
ceviche, 65
chat masala, 45
chicken:
    aromatic cold chicken, 49
    Bolivian corn pie, 68
    chicken satay, 44
    harira, 53
    jerked chicken, 69
    Moroccan spicy chicken, 56–7
    with noodles, 39

chilies, 16–19
chili flakes, 17
chili oil, 18
chili powder, 17
cilantro, 21
cinnamon, 20
cloves, 25
coconut, creamed, 42
cookies, gingerbread, 64
coriander, 21
corn pie, Bolivian, 68
country terrine, 59
couscous:
    almond couscous, 57
    fish couscous, 55
cubeb, 34
cumin, 23
curries:
    beef curry, 42–3
    vegetable curry, 46–7
curry leaves, 28
curry pastes, Thai, 41
curry powder, 47

D
dill, 13
dirty rice, Louisiana, 67
dry-roasting spices, 11

E
Europe, 58–64

F
falafel, 54
Far East, 38–44
fennel, 26
fenugreek, 36

fish:
    ceviche, 65
    fish couscous, 55
    sea bass with star anise, 40
    spicy fish stew, 50–1
five-spice powder, 40, 41
four-spices see quatre épices
freezing spices, 12
fruit chat, 45

G
galangal, 28
garam masala, 48, 49
garnishes, chilies, 19
ginger, 37
gingerbread cookies, 64
green curry paste, 41
grinding spices, 10

H
harira, 53
harissa, 52, 53
    with fish couscous, 55

I
India, 45–51
Indian date see tamarind

J
Jamaica pepper see allspice
Jamaican jerk seasoning, 69
jerked chicken, 69
juniper, 27
    potatoes with, 61

K
kaffir lime, 21
kitchen pepper, 11

L
lemongrass, 24
   Thai shrimp soup with, 38
lime pickle, 48
Louisiana dirty rice, 67

M
mace, 29
marinated shrimp, 66
marinated fish see ceviche
Middle East, 52–7
mixed spice, 63, 64
mixed vegetable curry, 46–7
Moroccan spicy chicken, 56–7
mulled wine, 63
mushrooms à la grecque, 60–1
mussel soup with saffron, 58
mustard, 14–15
mustard fruits, 14
mustard oil, 14

N
nigella, 30
noodles, chicken with, 39
North Africa, 52–7
nutmeg, 29

O
oil, chili, 18
oil, mustard, 14
olives, spiced, 54
onion seeds, black see nigella

P
paprika, 19
peanut sauce, 44
pepper, 32–3
   kitchen pepper, 11
   venison with green peppercorns, 62
pickle, lime, 48
poppy seeds, 31
pork:
   country terrine, 59
potatoes with juniper, 61
pudding spice see mixed spice

Q–R
quatre épices, 63
ras el hanout, 52, 53
red curry paste, Thai, 41
rice, Louisiana dirty, 67

S
safflower, 22
saffron, 22
   mussel soup with, 58
sansho, 36
satay, chicken, 44
sea bass with star anise, 40
sesame, 34–5
seven-spice powder, 39
   chicken with noodles, 39
shichimi togarashi see seven-spice powder
shrimp:
   marinated shrimp, 66
   Thai shrimp soup with lemongrass, 38
Sichuan pepper, 36
soups:
   harira, 53
   mussel soup with saffron, 58
   Thai shrimp soup with lemongrass, 38
spiced olives, 54
spiced vinegar, 30
spicy fish stew, 50–1
star anise, 27
   sea bass with, 40
storing spices, 11–12
sumac, 34

T
Tabasco sauce, 17
tahini, 34
tamarind, 34–5
taste, 9
terrine, country, 59
Thai shrimp soup with lemongrass, 38
Thai red curry paste, 41, 42
turmeric, 23

V
vanilla, 36
vegetables:
   mushrooms à la grecque, 60–1
   potatoes with juniper, 61
   vegetable curry, 46–7
venison with green peppercorns, 62
vinegar, spiced, 30

W
wine, mulled, 63

ACKNOWLEDGMENTS

Dorling Kindersley would like to thank Hilary Bird for
compiling the index, Alison Copland for proofreading,
Richard Hammond for editorial assistance, Robert Campbell
and Mark Bracey for DTP assistance, The Cheltenham
Kitchener for the loan of props, and Emma Patmore for testing
recipes and preparing food for special photography.

Photography
KEY: t *top*; b *bottom*; c *center*; l *left*; r *right*
Special food photography by Clive Streeter, assisted by Amy Hearn:
3, 6b, 7, 10, 11c & b, 12t, 12cl & cr, 14b, 15, 22b, 24bl,
37bl, bc, & br, 38, 39c & b, 40b, 45b, 49b, 53, 54,
55, 57b, 58, 61, 62, 65, 66t, 67, 68, 69b, 72.
All other photographs by Peter Chadwick,
David Murray/Jules Selmes, and Martin Norris.